Make Your Own Comics

Copyright © 2020 by Panel Meister Press
All rights reserved. This book or any portion thereof
may not be reproduced or used in any manner whatsoever
without the express written permission of the publisher
except for the use of brief quotations in a book review.

Printed in the United States of America
9798576070152

ELEMENTS

Here you will find ideas to make your comic book panels come to life!

SPEECH BUBBLES

For use when someone is speaking aloud.

THOUGHT BALLONS

Used when someone is thinking something to themselves.

NARRATION BOXES

Used to describe the scene of the panel or provide additional information.

SOUND EFFECTS

Want to make your pages more dynamic? Try adding sound effects!

SAMPLE PAGES

Want to get started but just don't know how? Check out these cool sample pages to get your ideas going!

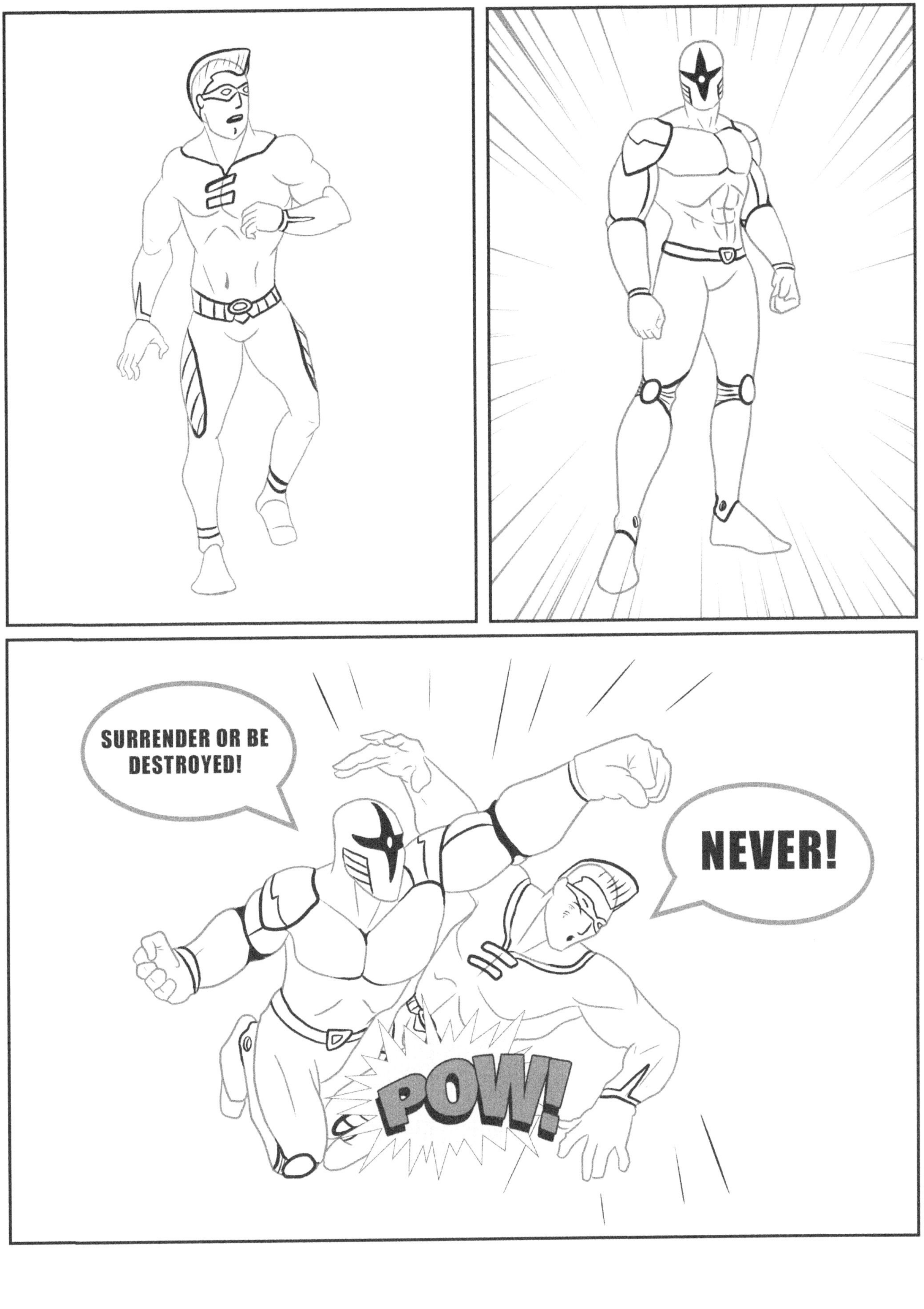

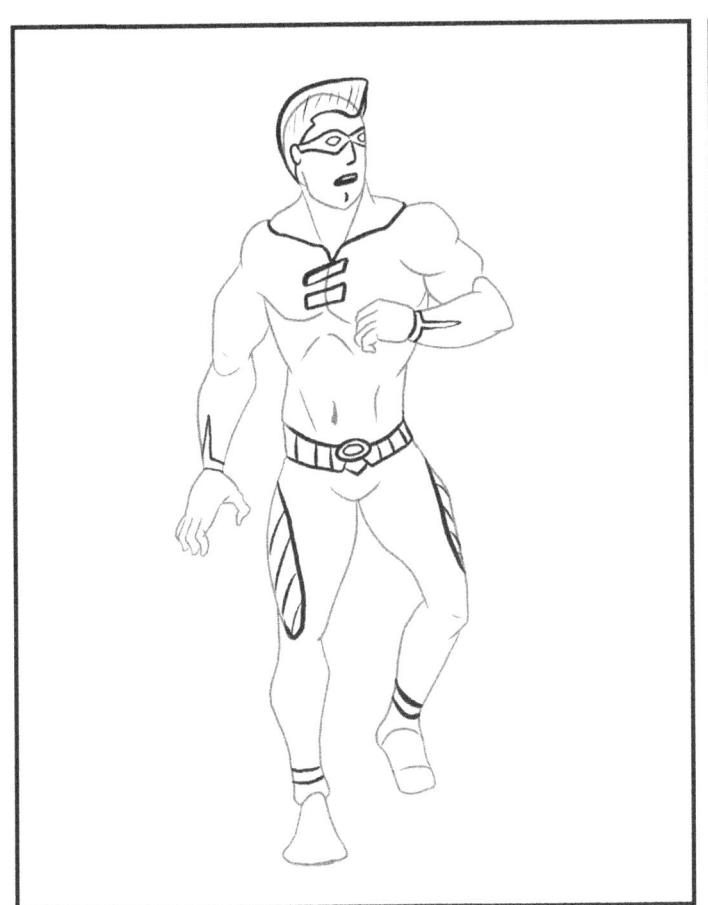
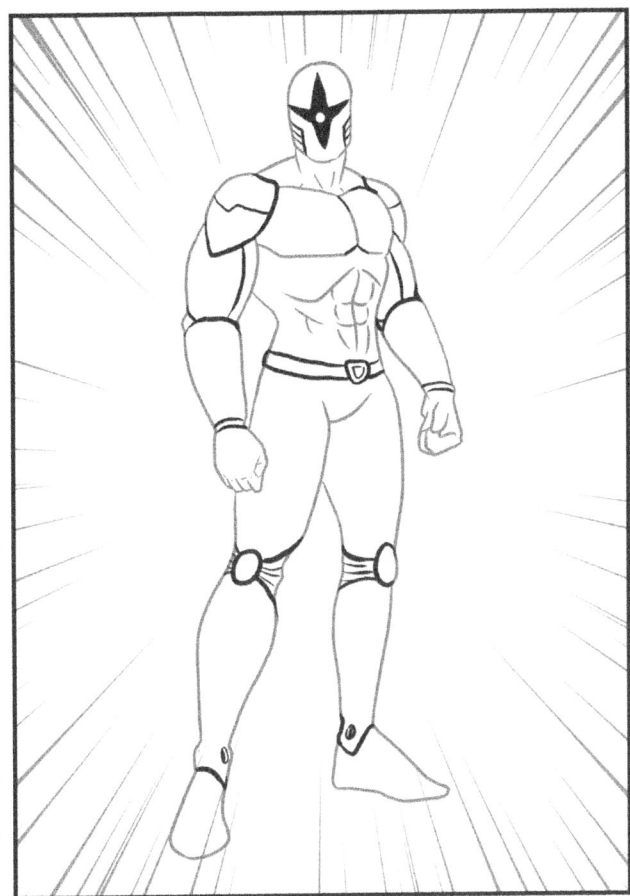

PRE-DRAWN TEMPLATES

Now that you have seen some examples, try to create your own adventures using the pre-drawn templates.

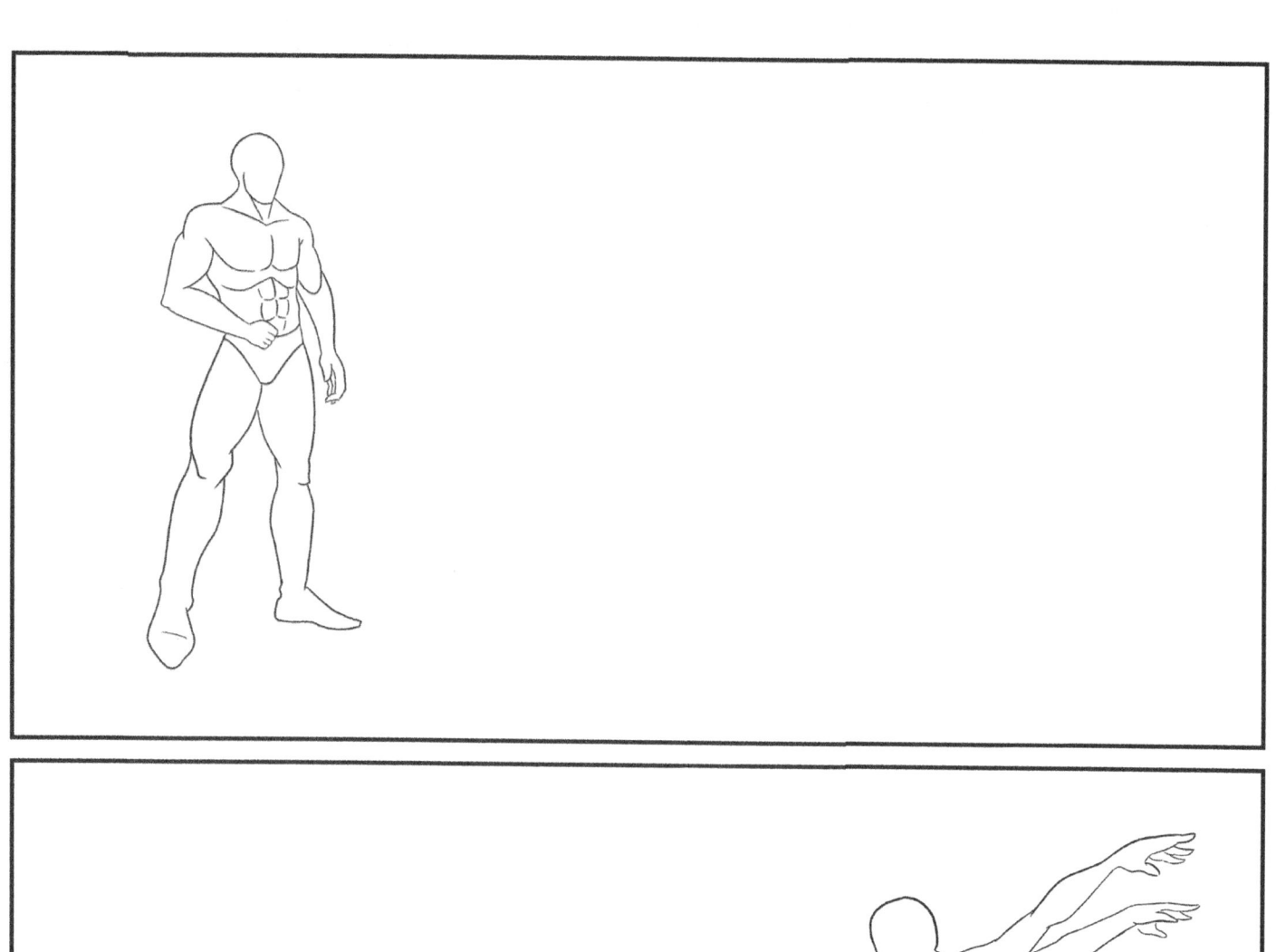

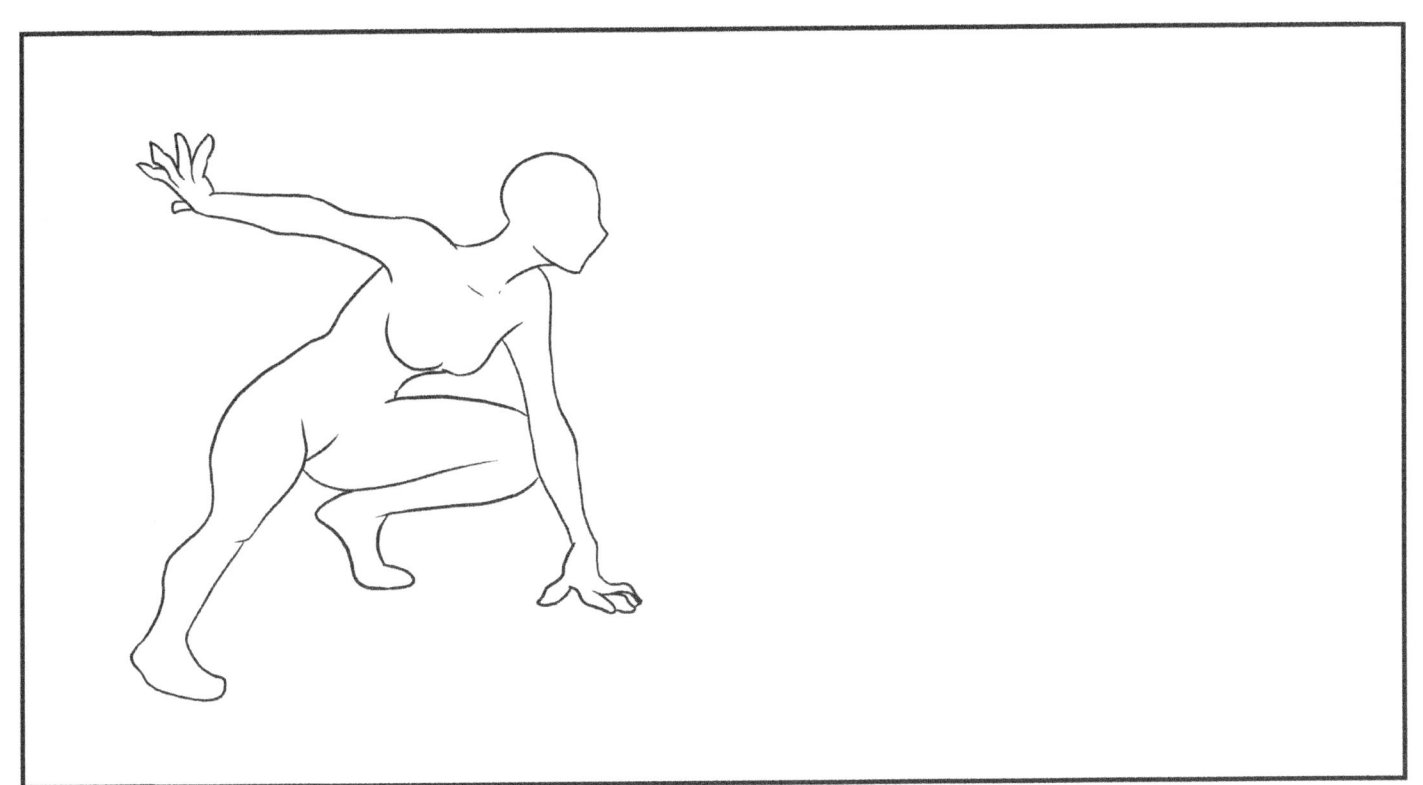

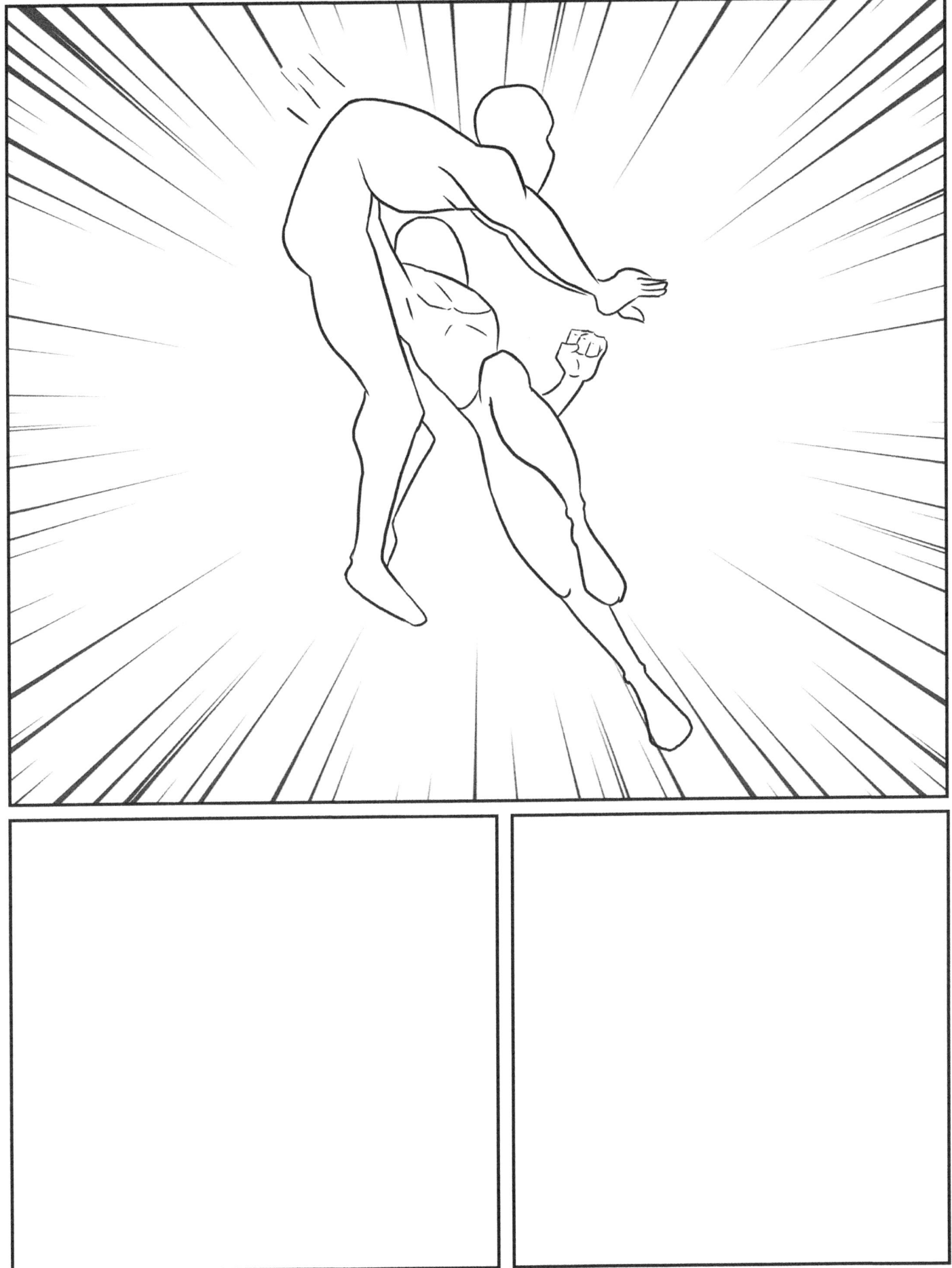

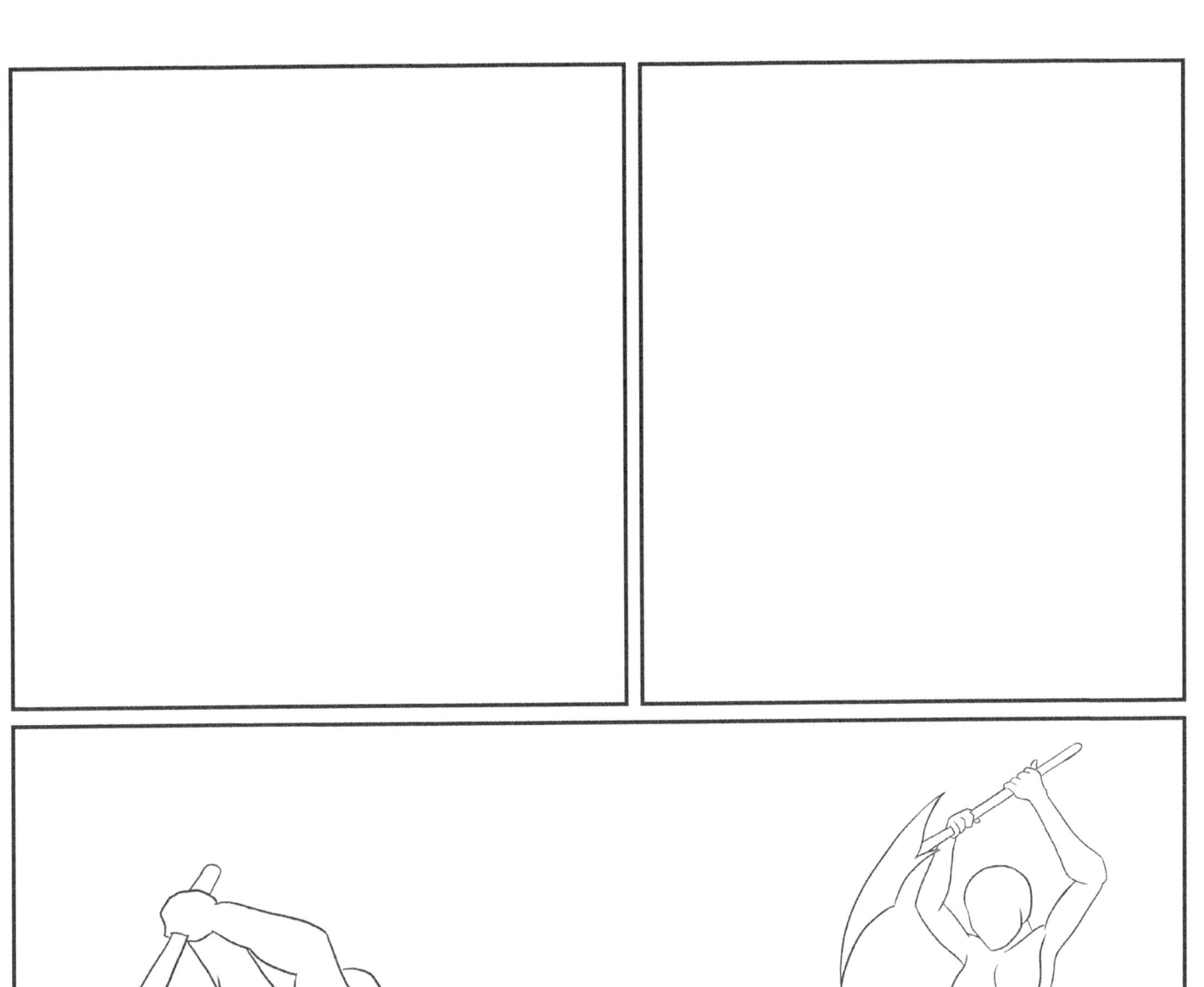

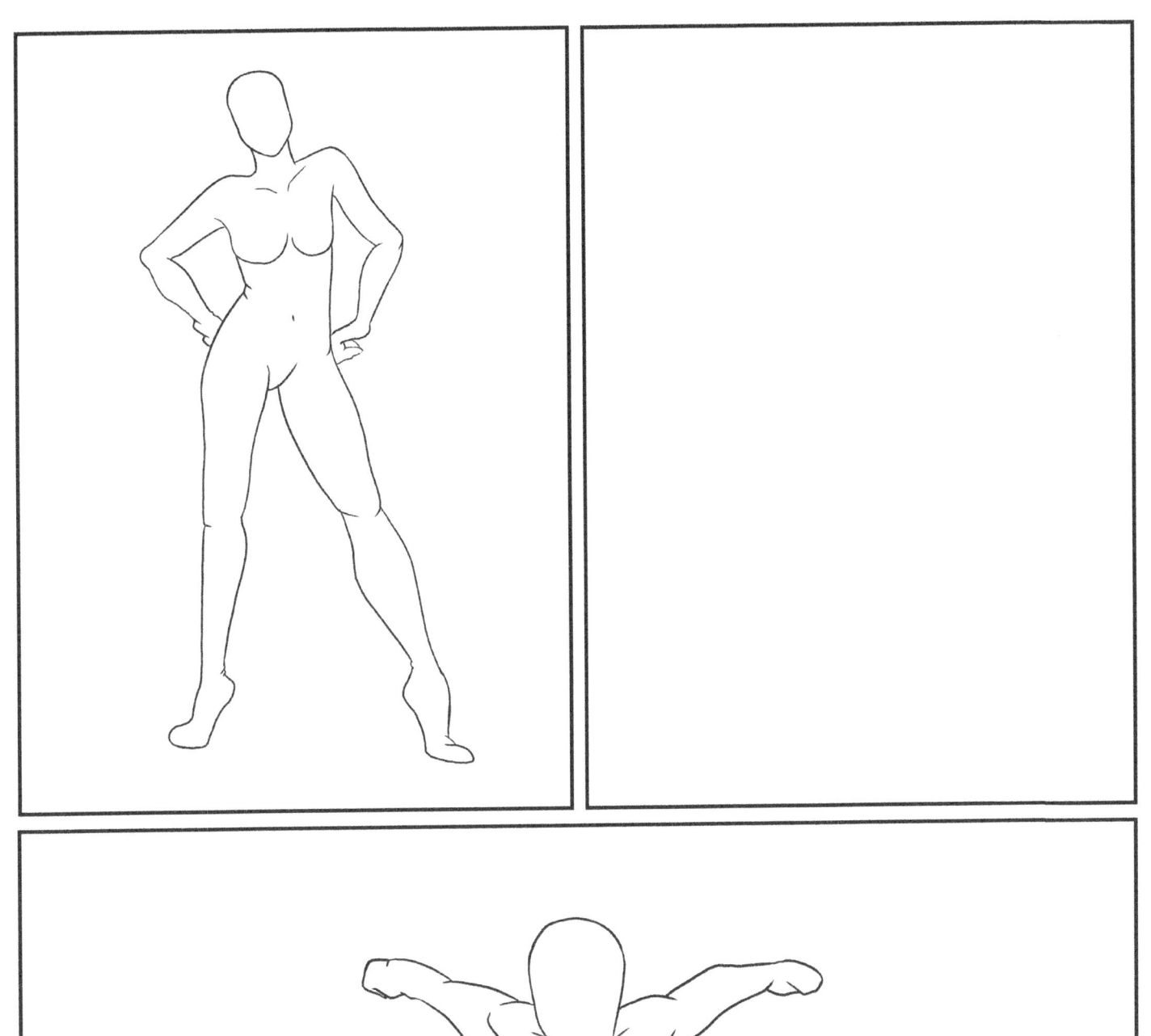

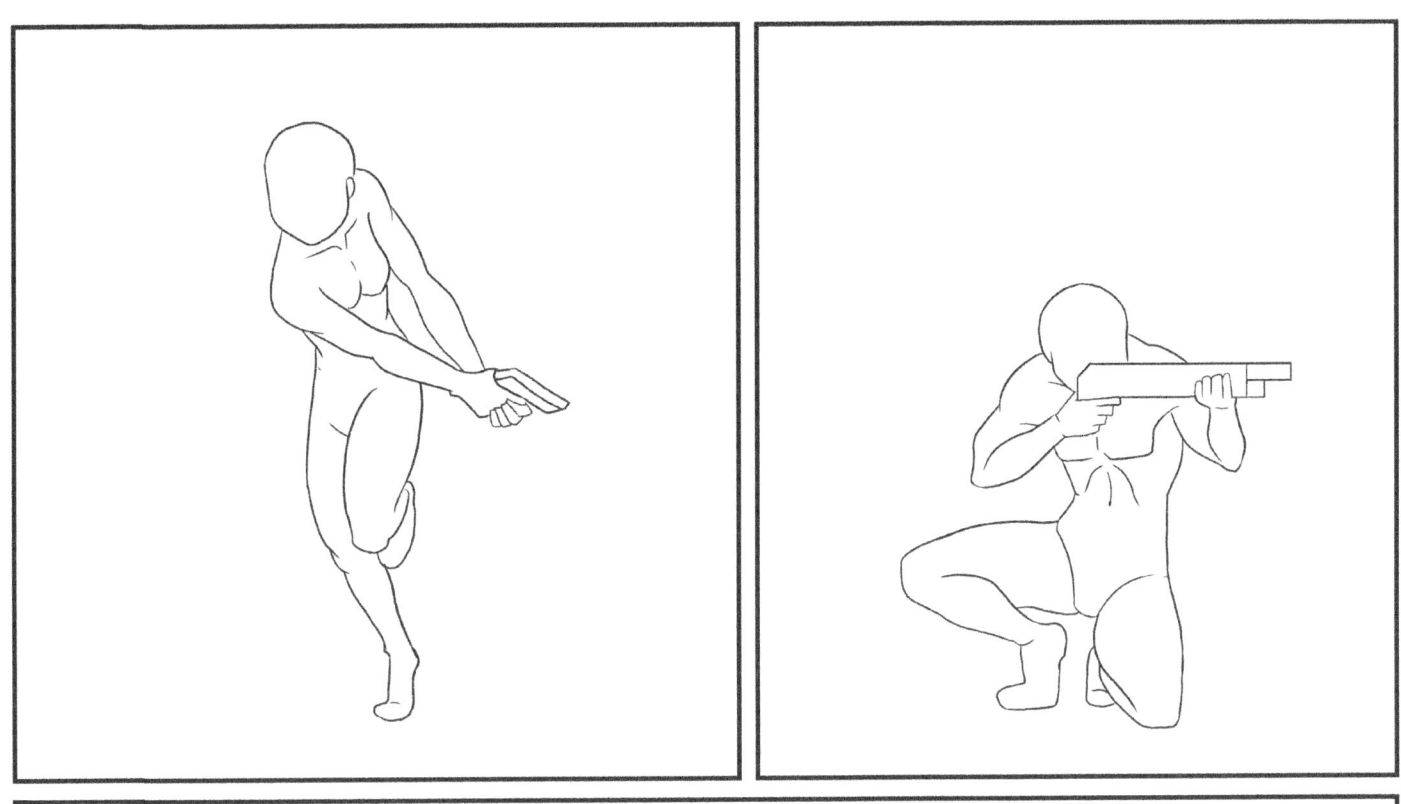

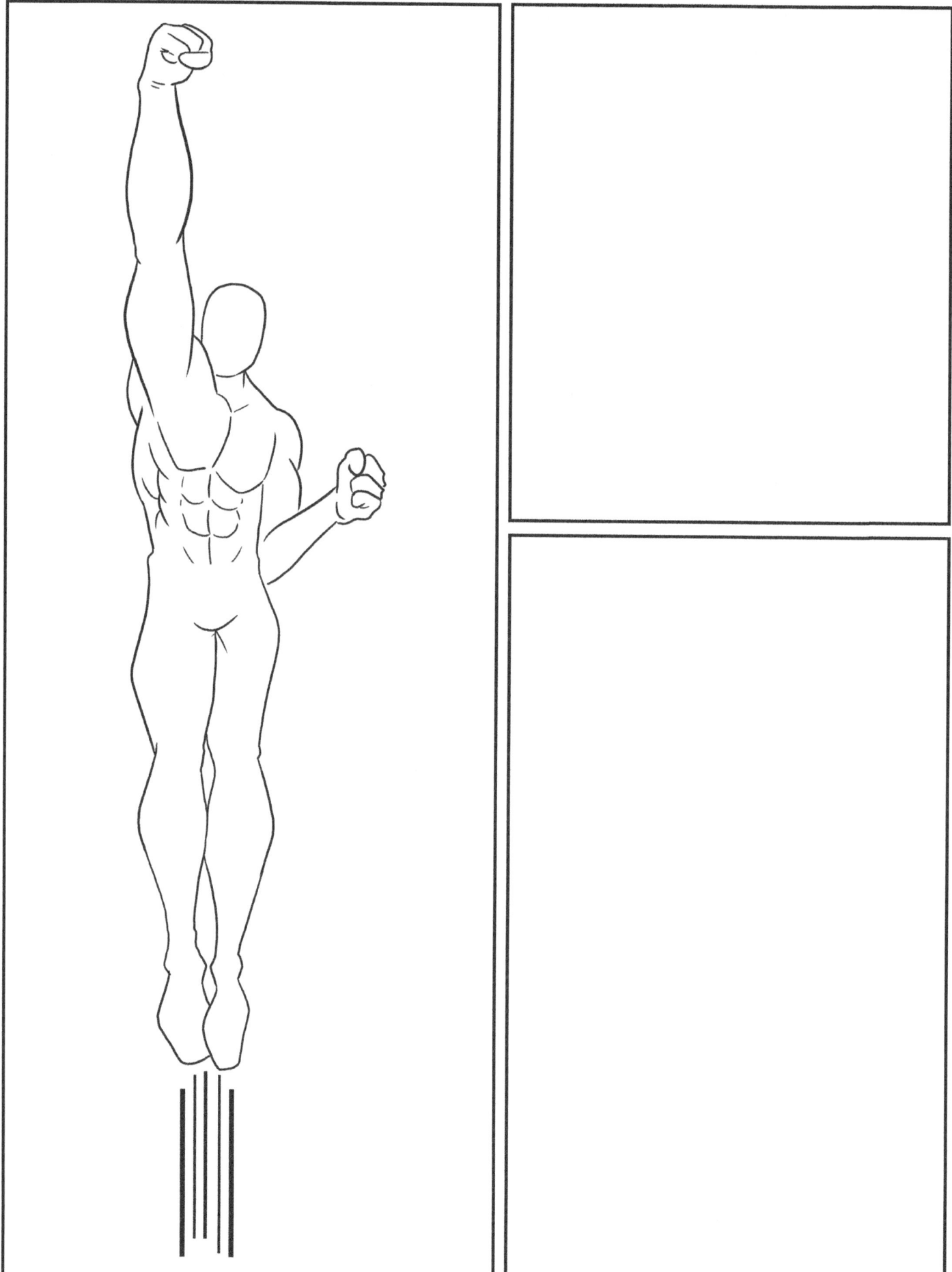

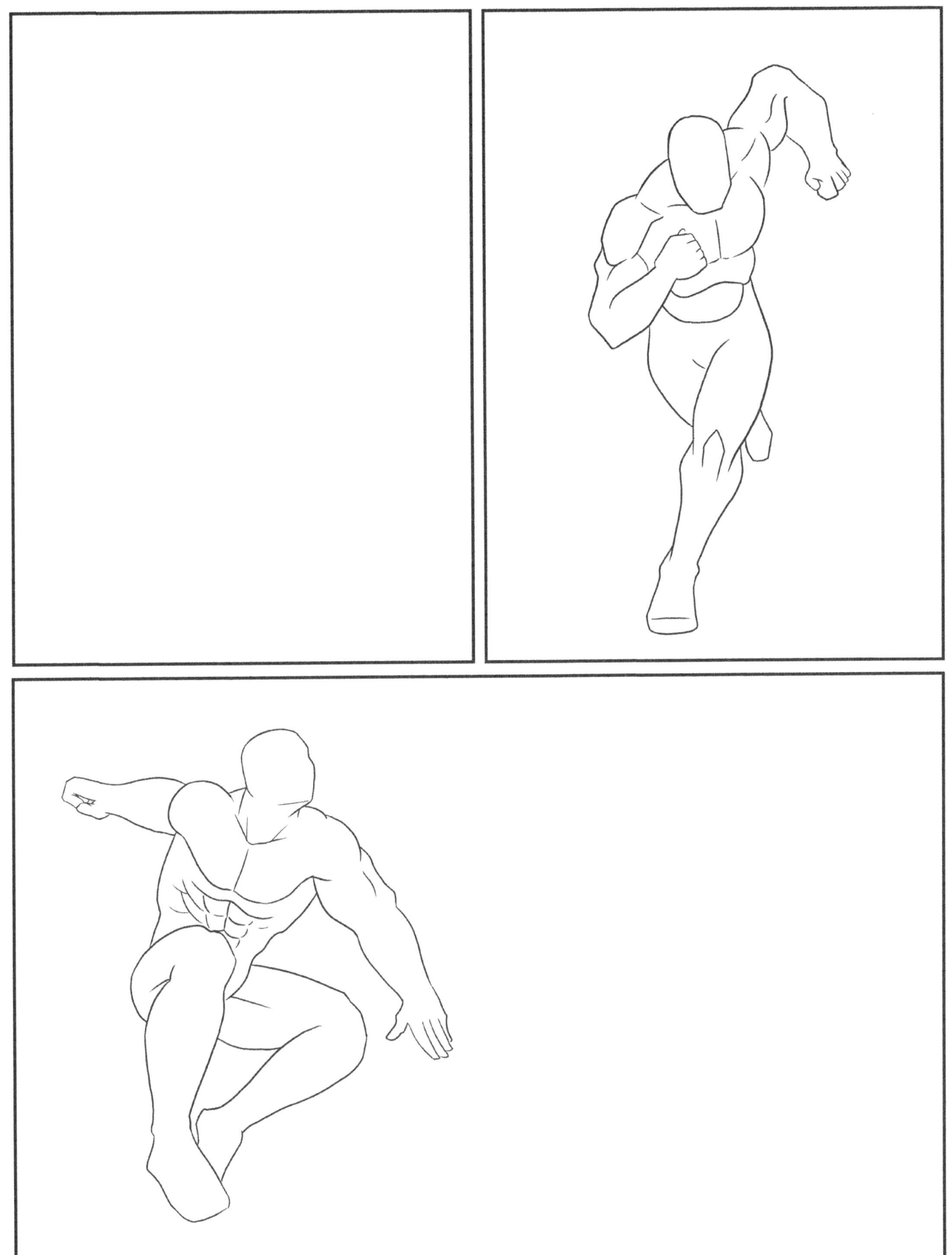

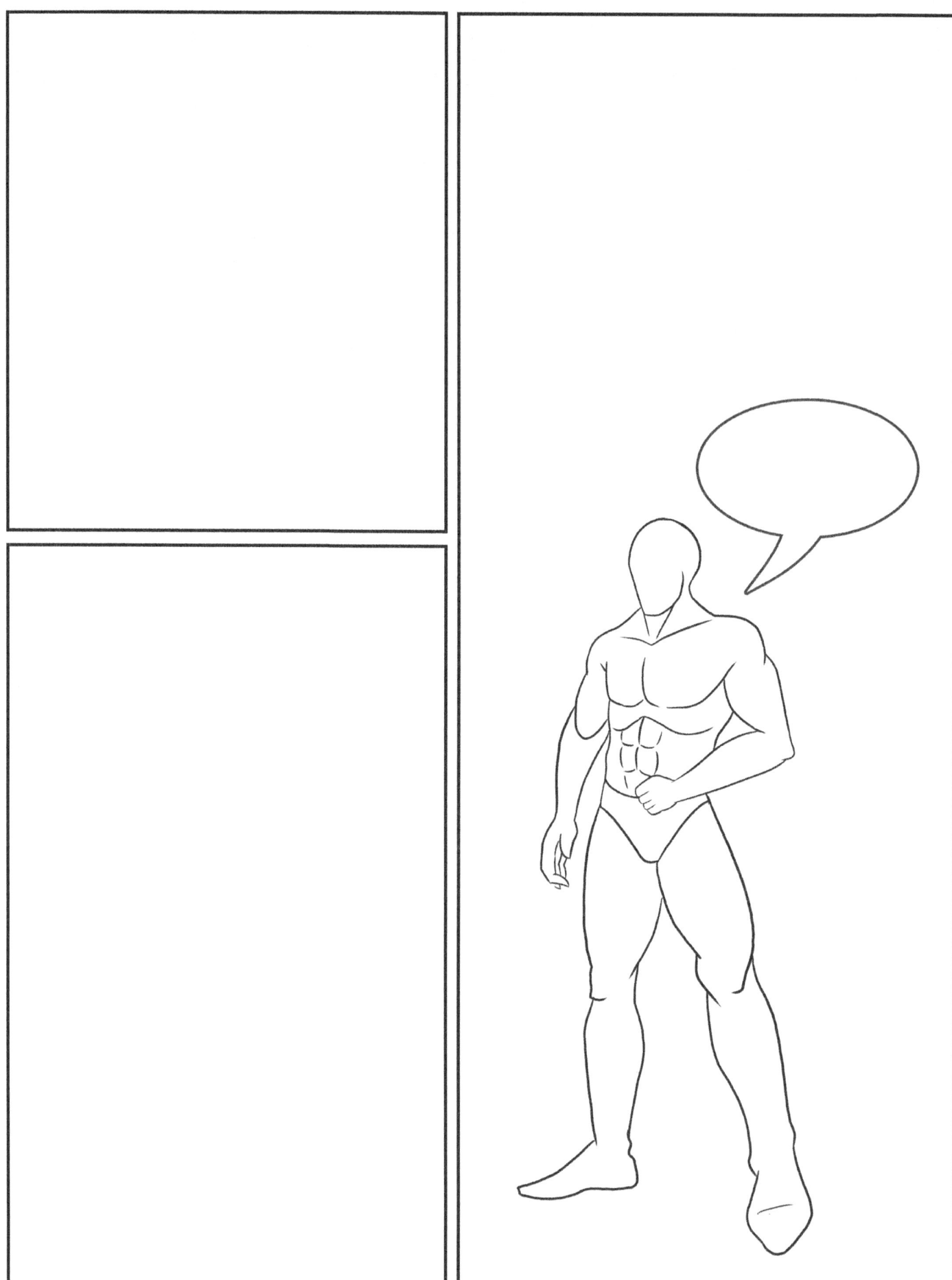

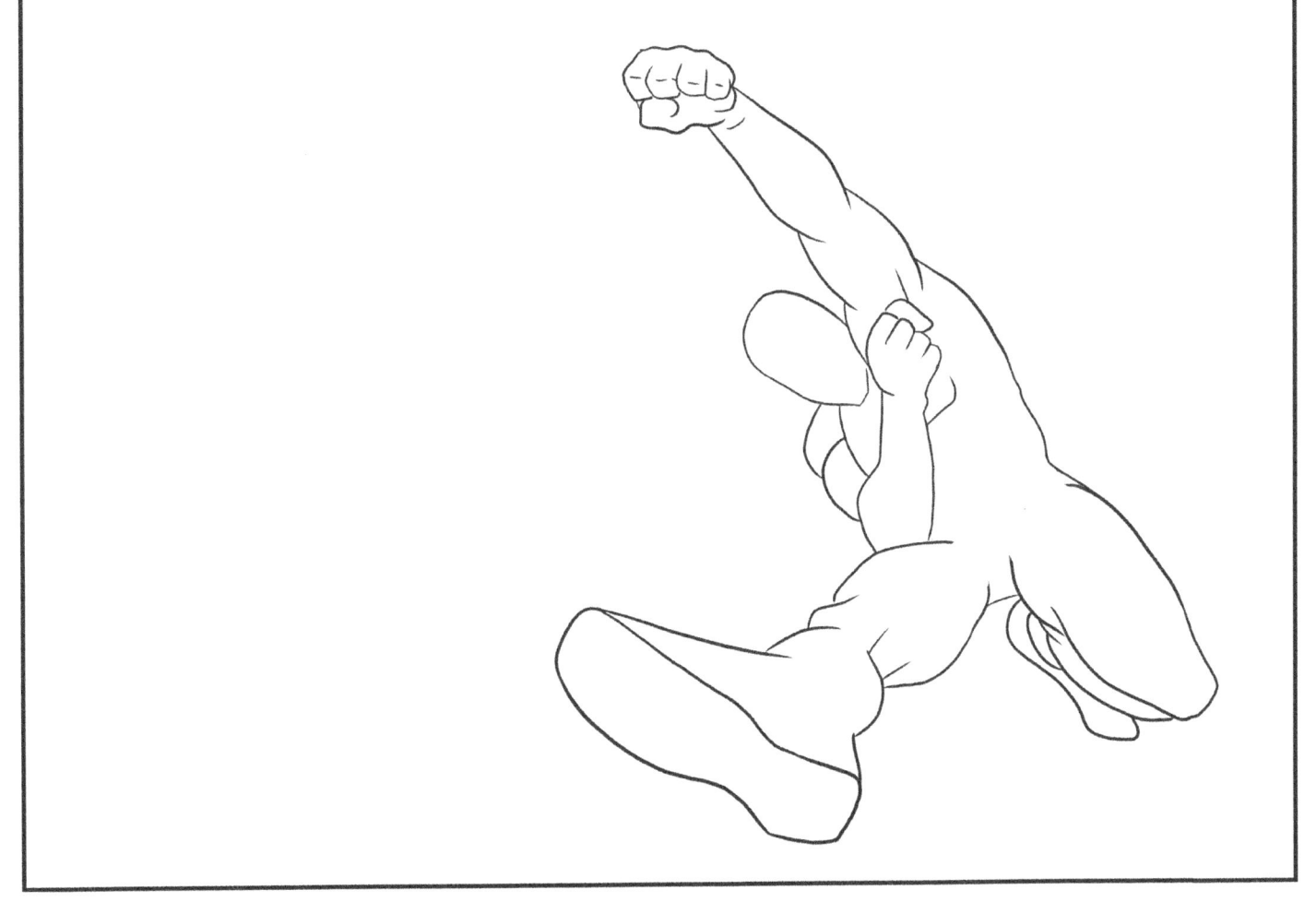

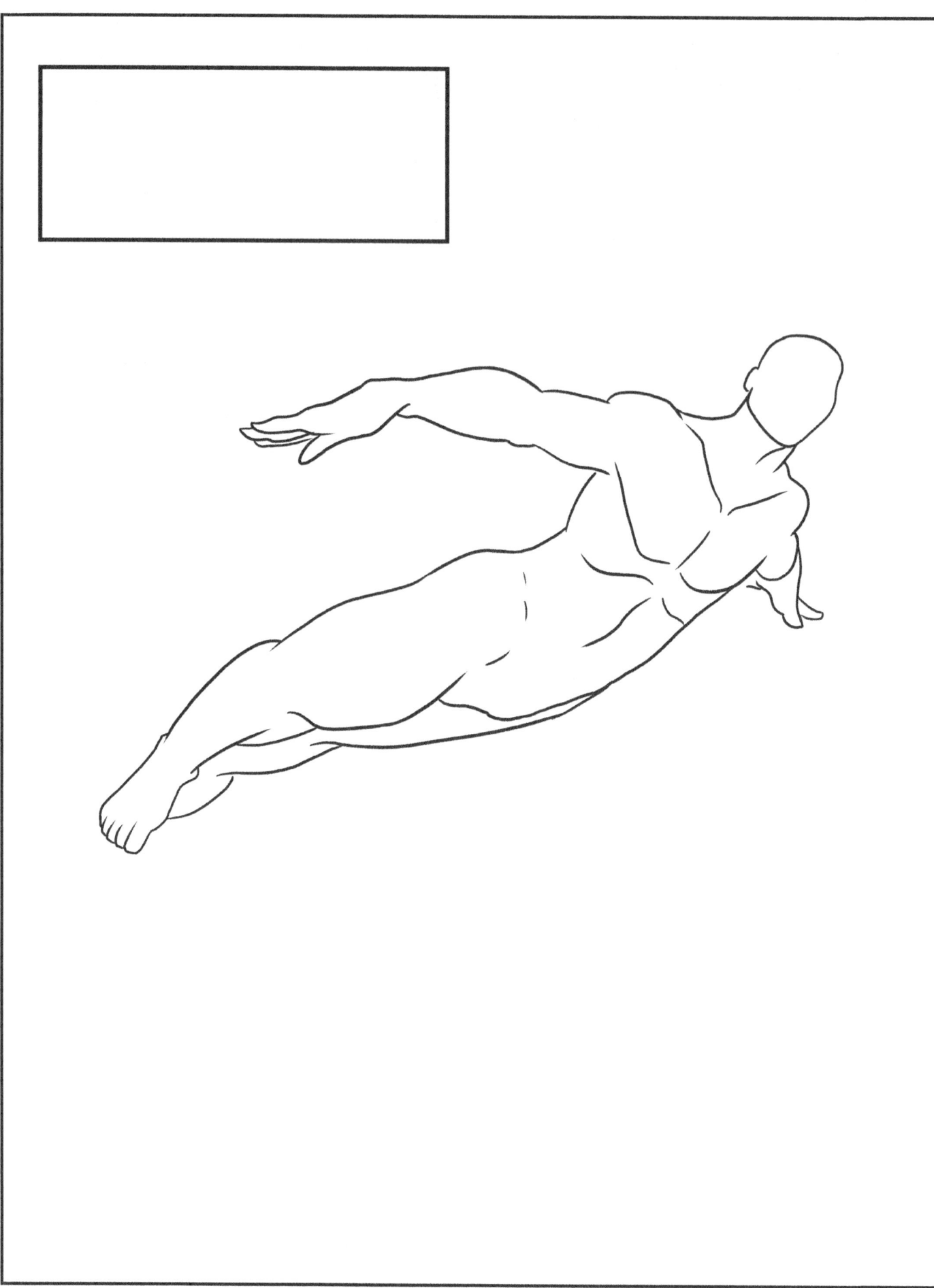

NOW IT'S YOUR TURN!

Now that you have had a chance to play around with the pre-drawn templates, it's time for you to unleash your own creativity! Use the reference pages and let your imagination run wild!

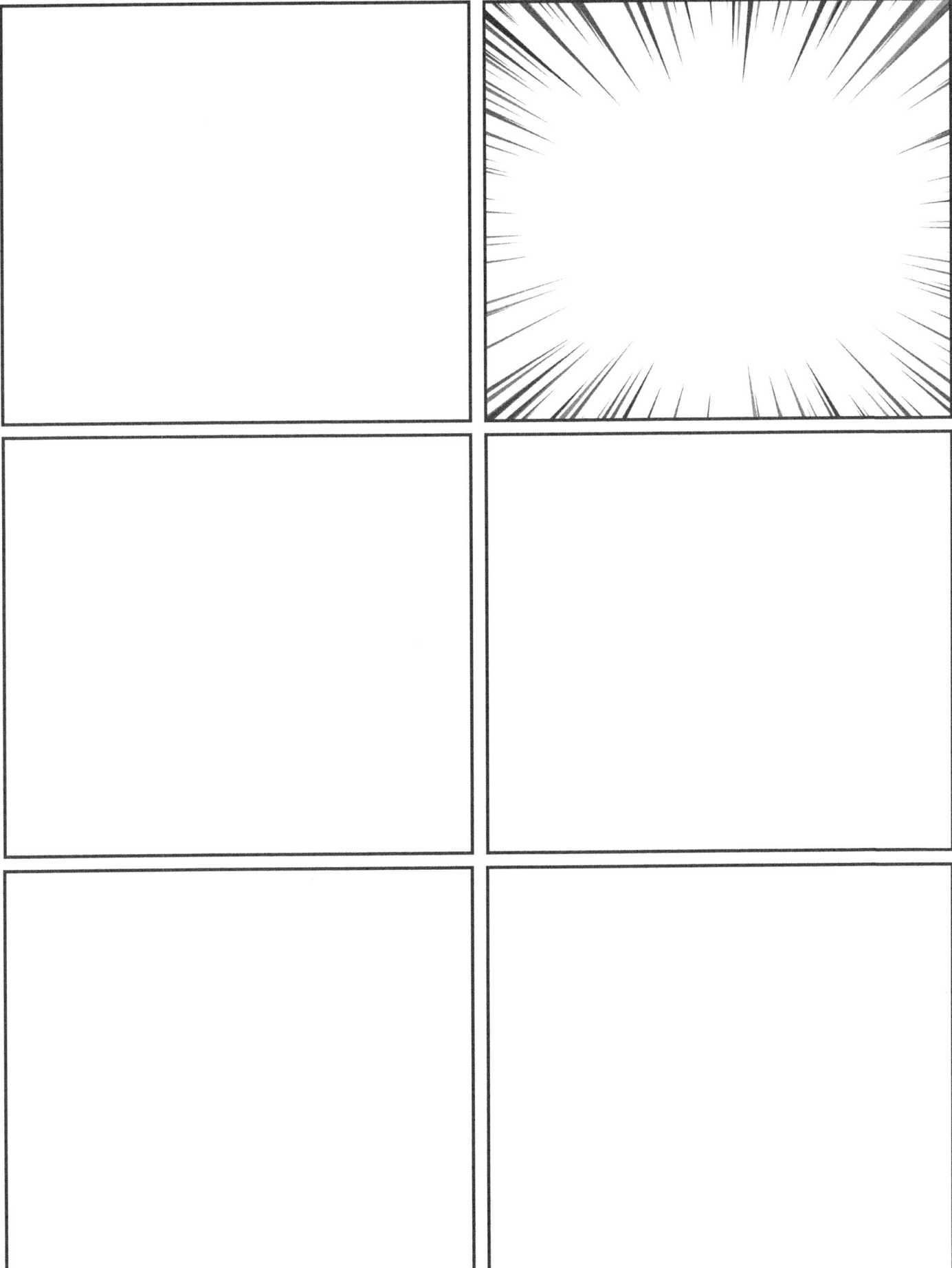

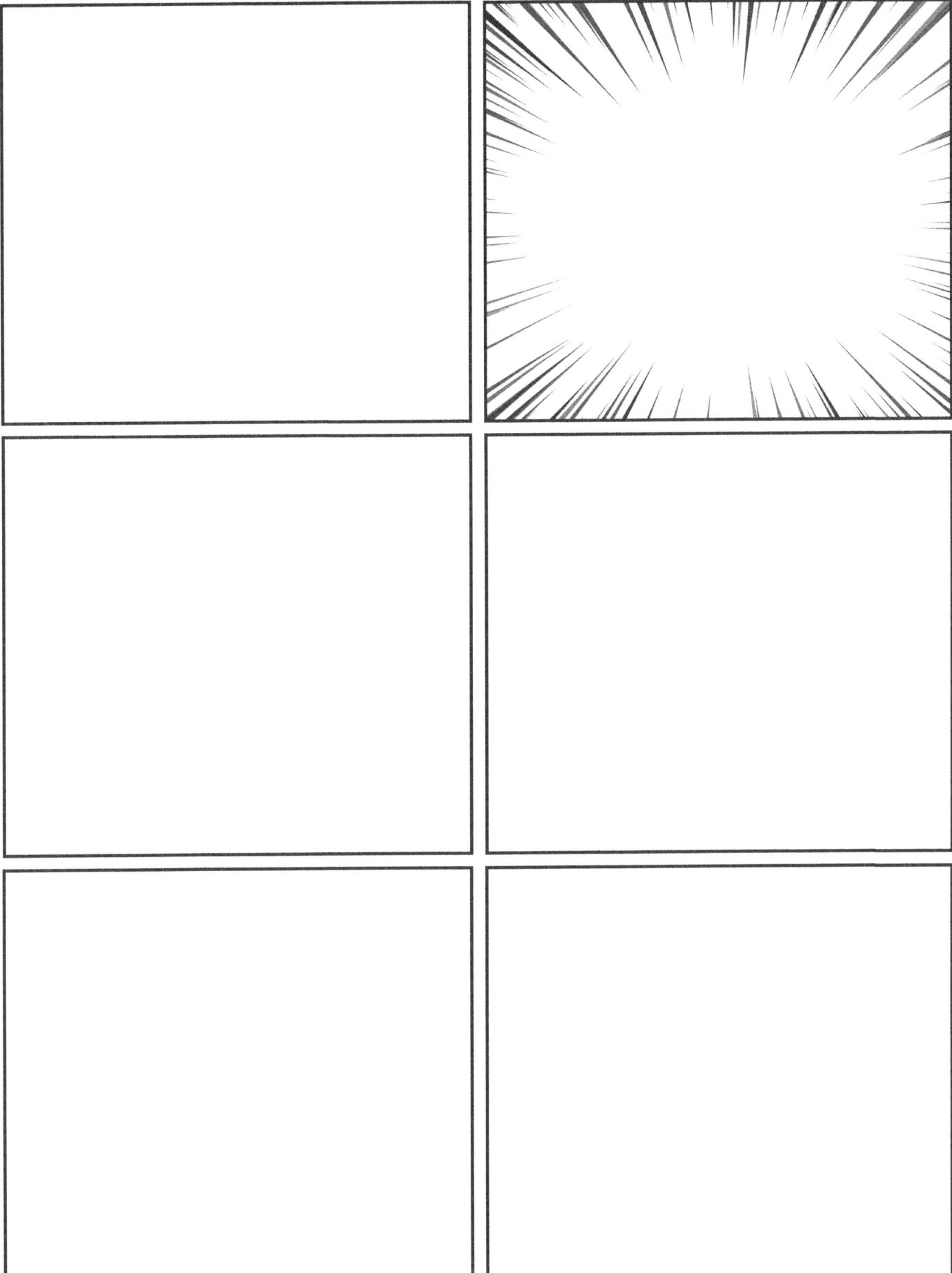

THANK YOU FOR YOUR PURCHASE!

We greatly appreciate your support. Without you, none of this would be possible. Please consider leaving us a review on Amazon. Reviews greatly help us to be able to continue to produce books such as this one.

Made in the USA
Monee, IL
19 December 2021